DEBATES ON THE RISE OF ISLAMIST EXTREMISM

Robert Green

ReferencePoint
Press®

San Diego, CA

For more information, contact:
ReferencePoint Press, Inc.
PO Box 27779
San Diego, CA 92198
www.ReferencePointPress.com

LIBRARY OF CONGRESS CATALOGING-IN-PUBLICATION DATA

Name: Green, Robert, 1969– author.
Title: Debates on the Rise of Islamist Extremism/by Robert Green.
Description: San Diego, CA: ReferencePoint Press, Inc., [2018] | Series:
  Debating History | Includes bibliographical references and index.
Identifiers: LCCN 2018017503 (print) | LCCN 2018018423 (ebook) | ISBN
  9781682823729 (eBook) | ISBN 9781682823712 (hardback)
Subjects: LCSH: Religious fanaticism—Islam. | Religious
  fanaticism—Islam—History.
Classification: LCC BP190.5.R43 (ebook) | LCC BP190.5.R43 G74 2018 (print) |
  DDC 320.55/7—dc23
LC record available at https://lccn.loc.gov/2018017503

Contents

Is slavery immoral?

No thinking person today would argue that slavery is moral. Yet in the United States in the early and mid-1800s, slavery was an accepted institution in the southern states. While many southerners never owned slaves, the institution of slavery had widespread support from plantation owners, elected officials, and even the general populace. Its defenders were often respected members of their communities. For instance, John C. Calhoun—a US senator from South Carolina—was a staunch defender of slavery. He believed that enslaved Africans benefited from their status as slaves—and said as much during an 1837 Senate speech. "Never before," he stated, "has the black race of Central Africa, from the dawn of history to the present day, attained a condition so civilized and so improved, not only physically, but morally and intellectually."

Statements like this might be confounding and hurtful today. But a true understanding of history—especially of those events that have altered daily life and human communities—requires students to become familiar with the thoughts, attitudes, and beliefs of the people who lived these events. Only by examining various perspectives will students truly understand the past and be able to make sound judgments about the future.

This is the goal of the *Debating History* series. Through a narrative-driven, pro/con format, the series introduces students to some of the complex issues that have dominated public discourse over the decades—topics such as the slave trade, twentieth-century immigration, the Soviet Union's collapse, and the rise of Islamist extremism. All chapters revolve around a single, pointed question, such as the following:

- Is slavery immoral?
- Do immigrants threaten American culture and values?
- Did the arms race cause the Soviet Union's collapse?
- Does poverty cause Islamist extremism?

This inquiry-based approach to history introduces student researchers to core issues and concerns on a given topic. Each chapter includes one part that argues the affirmative and one part that argues the negative—all written by a single author. With the single-author format, the predominant arguments for and against an issue can be synthesized into clear, accessible discussions supported by details and evidence, including relevant facts, quotes, and examples. All volumes include focus questions to guide students as they read each pro/con discussion, a visual chronology, and a list of sources for conducting further research.

This approach reflects the guiding principles set out in the College, Career, and Civic Life (C3) Framework for Social Studies State Standards developed by the National Council for the Social Studies. "History is interpretive," the framework's authors write. "Even if they are eyewitnesses, people construct different accounts of the same event, which are shaped by their perspectives—their ideas, attitudes, and beliefs. Historical understanding requires recognizing this multiplicity of points of view in the past. . . . It also requires recognizing that perspectives change over time, so that historical understanding requires developing a sense of empathy with people in the past whose perspectives might be very different from those of today." The *Debating History* series supports these goals by providing a solid introduction to the study of pro/con issues in history.

Important Events in the Rise of Islamist Extremism

1989
Soviet troops withdraw from Afghanistan.

1928
Hassan al-Banna founds the Muslim Brotherhood in Egypt.

1979
Soviet troops invade Afghanistan.

1940   1950   1960   1970   1980   1990

1964
Ayatollah Ruhollah Khomeini is exiled from Iran.

1979
The shah flees Iran; the Islamic Republic of Iran is founded.

1990
US forces embark on a campaign to drive Iraqi troops out of Kuwait in the Gulf War.

1991
The Soviet Union collapses, ending the Cold War.

1996
Osama bin Laden declares war on the United States.

2001
Terrorists attack the United States on September 11; US forces invade Afghanistan on October 7; the USA PATRIOT Act is signed into law on October 26.

2011
Osama bin Laden is killed by US special forces in Pakistan.

2014
The Islamic State in Iraq and Syria (ISIS) proclaims the founding of a caliphate, or Islamic State, that stretches across parts of Iraq and Syria.

2004
Islamist terrorists kill 190 people with bombs on commuter trains in Madrid, Spain.

| 2000 | 2003 | 2006 | 2009 | 2012 | 2015 | 2018 |

2003
US forces invade Iraq and overthrow Iraqi dictator Saddam Hussein.

2012
Mohamed Morsi of the Muslim Brotherhood is elected president of Egypt.

2005
Islamist terrorists detonate bombs in London's subway system.

2017
ISIS is driven out of Iraq and its last major stronghold in Syria.

2006
The leader of al Qaeda in Iraq, Abu Musab al-Zarqawi, is killed by US forces.

7

Chapter One

A Brief History of Islamist Extremism

When Egypt's prime minister, Mahmud Fahmi al-Nuqrashi, arrived at work on the morning of December 28, 1948, an assassin was waiting. This was Abdel Meguid Ahmed Hassan, a twenty-one-year-old medical student who had disguised himself in the black uniform of an Egyptian police officer and was standing guard near the elevator that usually took the prime minister up to his office. As al-Nuqrashi approached, Hassan saluted, drew a pistol, and fired six times. The prime minister died shortly after.

At the time of the assassination, Egypt was bubbling with discontent. Many Egyptians hated Egypt's monarch, the rich socialite King Farouk, who was good at spending money but showed little interest in the problems of his people. Others resented Western interference in the kingdom and the modernization that Western ideas brought. Most of all they objected to the declining importance of religion.

Hassan, the assassin, was angry about all these things. It was later discovered that he was a member of the Muslim Brotherhood, an extremist organization that considers violence an acceptable means of restoring Islam to the center of political life in countries with large Muslim populations. When interviewed by the police, Hassan cited the government's outlawing of the Muslim Brotherhood as a chief reason for the assassination. "The Muslim Brotherhood," Hassan said, "had been the only organization fighting for Islam in the last twenty years."[1]

Society of Muslim Brothers

What made Hassan an Islamist was his belief that religion should determine the political life of Muslims. Not all Islamists are extremists, however. Some belong to peaceful political parties and sit in democratically elected legislatures. What made Hassan and many other Muslim Brothers Islamist extremists was their unwillingness to accept that people could have different ideas. They believed that only by restoring a rigid form of Islam could Egypt be great again. Although not all Islamists are violent, Islamist extremist groups have grown more violent over time.

The origins of Islamist extremism can be found in the teachings of Egyptian scholars in the early twentieth century, and its rise is closely associated with the history of the Society of Muslim Brothers, better known as the Muslim Brotherhood. When it was established in 1928, its founder, Hassan al-Banna, hoped to restore Islamic government peacefully. He hoped to rid Egypt of Western influence and reestablish religious government that had been a hallmark of early Islamic history. In his view it was immoral to separate religion from politics, and he objected to the separation of church and state found in Western societies. "If someone should say to you: This is politics!," al-Banna said, "say: This is Islam, and we do not recognize such divisions."[2]

The Cycle of Violence Begins

Al-Banna was opposed to the use of violence to achieve Islamist aims. Not all in the Muslim Brotherhood agreed with him, however. The use of violence was seen by Hassan and many other Muslim Brothers as the only way to achieve their ends. It was somewhat ironic therefore that al-Banna was gunned down in retribution for Hassan's assassination of Egypt's prime minister.

Without his restraining voice, his organization swung decisively in favor of armed struggle against the government. It also found a successor to head the organization who has inspired Islamist violence ever since.

When the Muslim Brotherhood attempted to assassinate another Egyptian leader, President Gamal Abdel Nasser, in 1954, the army arrested thousands of suspected Muslim Brothers. One of those arrested was Sayyid Qutb. An Islamic scholar and political activist, Qutb argued that Muslims who did not agree with the Muslim Brotherhood's views on Islam were the enemies of the Islamists. His lasting contribution to the Islamist movement was to justify, through his scholarly writings from the 1930s and 1940s, the use of violence against non-Muslims and against Muslims who did not agree with his strict interpretation of Islam. He advocated Islamist violence through holy war, or jihad, against all those who did not agree with the Islamists. "Pre-eminently among the pioneers of 20th-century Islamism, Sayyid Qutb has come to be seen as the evil genius who inspired today's global jihad,"[3] writes the *Economist*.

> "Some of the world's most dangerous terrorists were once Egyptian Muslim Brotherhood members."[4]
>
> —Journalist Jayshree Bajoria

For his role in the Nasser assassination attempt and refusal to renounce violence, Qutb was sentenced to death by hanging in 1966. But after his death, the influence of the Muslim Brotherhood continued to inspire terrorist groups. Among those who took their inspiration from the Muslim Brotherhood was al Qaeda, whose leader, Osama bin Laden, orchestrated the September 11, 2001, attacks on the United States. "The Brotherhood has spawned branches all across the globe," writes journalist Jayshree Bajoria. "In addition, some of the world's most dangerous terrorists were once Egyptian Muslim Brotherhood members."[4]

Revolution in Iran

In the history of Islamist extremism, the Muslim Brotherhood is an important example of a Sunni Islamist group—Islam's largest faction. But the second of Islam's two major factions, the Shia, has also produced Islamist extremism. This factional split in Islam arose after the death of Mohammad, Islam's prophet, in 632 CE. The two groups disagreed over who would speak for Islam after his death. No agreement was reached, and the two factions thus developed different traditions and a bitter rivalry within the Islamic world. Sunni Muslims account for about 85 percent of the Muslim world, and Shia Muslims account for most of the rest. The Shia account for the majority of the Muslim populations of only a few countries—Azerbaijan, Bahrain, Iran, Iraq, and Lebanon. But the Shia have played a large role in the history of Islamist extremism, primarily because of the rise of extremism in Iran.

In the 1970s the Iranian population was overwhelmingly against the nation's corrupt monarchy, headed by Mohammad

Reza Pahlavi, more commonly known as the shah. While the shah lived a lavish life of riches, his people suffered from high food prices and low wages. If they protested, they were subjected to beatings, imprisonment, or death.

As in Egypt, political opposition was voiced by religious leaders. Chief among them was Ayatollah Ruhollah Khomeini, who accused the shah of destroying Islamic traditions in Iran by siding too closely with the West and by reducing Islam's role in society. To quell dissent, the shah exiled Khomeini in 1964, but opposition to the shah continued to grow. In 1979, when the shah's soldiers opened fire on protesters, the Iranian public rose up against the government. The shah fled, and Khomeini returned from exile to a hero's welcome. He abolished the monarchy and declared the Islamic Republic of Iran—a government that was truly Islamist and wanted to spread Islamist extremism to other Shia communities.

Prisoners of the Ayatollah

Khomeini also signaled that foreigners, especially Westerners who had supported the shah (a group that included the US government), were no longer welcome in Iran. "I beg to God to cut off the hand of all evil foreigners and all their helpers in Iran,"[5] Khomeini said on the day he returned to Iran.

Khomeini's desire to punish the West for its past support of the shah was put on full display when Islamist students stormed the US embassy on November 4, 1979. For 444 days, fifty-two US diplomats and military personnel were held hostage. TV coverage ensured that the entire world witnessed a new phase of Islamist extremism, both hostile to the West and willing to use violence against its enemies.

Khomeini's combination of Islamic fundamentalism and revolutionary fervor signaled a new international threat. "To Americans, the hostage crisis was an unprovoked, inexcusable crime, carried out by a scruffy band of half-crazy Islamist zealots driven by a senseless hatred of all things American," writes journalist Mark

Bowden. "It was America's first modern encounter with hostile Islamists, and the first time Americans heard their country called 'the Great Satan.'"[6]

A Global Threat

Since its rise in both the Sunni and Shia communities, Islamist extremism has continued to grow. The Islamists themselves see the world as divided into enemies from two camps. In the first camp are the secular governments in the Islamic world. Islamists identify this as the near enemy—the enemy at home. In the second camp are Western governments that back those secular, usually pro-Western governments. Those governments, chiefly the United States and European nations, are known as the far enemy.

Westerners often view Islamist terrorism as predominantly anti-Western, mostly because they are watching news reports of terrorist attacks in their own countries. But the violence of the Islamist extremist movement has disproportionately affected Muslims. "Muslims suffered between 82 and 97% of terrorism-related fatalities over the past five years,"[7] concluded a 2011 report by the US government's National Counterterrorism Center.

But that violence has also often spilled out of the Islamic world as Islamists have taken their violent struggle abroad. In Europe they have detonated bombs in London's subway system and on Spain's railways, bombed train stations in Belgium, and conducted shooting sprees in France. Their targets have overwhelmingly been civilians, and their attacks are meant to provoke a reaction from Western governments.

> "To Americans, the hostage crisis was an unprovoked, inexcusable crime. . . . It was America's first modern encounter with hostile Islamists, and the first time Americans heard their country called 'the Great Satan.'"[6]
>
> —Journalist Mark Bowden

13

When Islamist extremists, for example, used four commercial airplanes to attack the United States on September 11, 2001, the world responded with a global war on terror. The felling of the twin skyscrapers known as the World Trade Center and the partial destruction of the Pentagon, the center of US military power, sparked a war that continues today. That global war has spread the appeal of violent extremism. Since 2001 Islamism has become a worldwide phenomenon as reflected by the number of groups that antiterrorism forces are fighting. "American service members have been deployed in a war that has gradually stretched to jihadist groups that did not exist in 2001 and now operate across distant parts of the world," noted the *New York Times* in 2018.[8]

Since sprouting up in Egypt as a largely local phenomenon, Islamist extremism has spread around the globe. Today it presents a challenge both to peaceful Muslims and to those nations fighting extremism and the violence it produces.

Chapter Two

Is Islamist Extremism the Result of Political Repression?

Islamist Extremism Is a Direct Result of Political Repression

- Political repression led to radicalization.
- The exclusion of Islamist politicians from political participation resulted in radicalization.
- Mass arrests galvanized extremism, and jails became recruiting grounds for Islamists.

The Debate at a Glance

Political Repression Is Not the Main Cause of Islamist Extremism

- Islamism is an ideology that arose without repression.
- Islamists have waged violent struggles even when not repressed.
- Islamist ideology leads to intolerance even when Islamists are in power.

Islamist Extremism Is a Direct Result of Political Repression

"Terrorism flourishes in places where the government is no longer seen as being on the side of the people."

—Lauren Kosa, former US State Department official

Lauren Kosa, "Dictators Don't Stabilize the Middle East. They Just Create More Terrorists," *Washington Post*, April 13, 2016. www.washingtonpost.com.

Consider these questions as you read:

1. Why did the Muslim Brotherhood change from a peaceful organization fighting for the rights of Egyptians to a violent terrorist group?
2. Do you think that the use of violence to end oppression is ever justified? Why or why not?
3. Why would opposition to the governments of Egypt and Iran arise in the mosques of those countries?

Editor's note: The discussion that follows presents common arguments made in support of this perspective. All arguments are supported by facts, quotes, and examples taken from various sources of the period or present day.

Islamist extremists share a powerful common narrative. They feel that the societies in which they live are unjust. While the few control a country's wealth, the majority suffer in poverty.

Historically, however, when Islamists took to the streets to protest corruption, they were beaten and imprisoned. In the societies in which Islamist extremism arose, voices of dissent were not tolerated. The political system was closed to the protesters, who were not allowed to participate in elections and therefore had no way to change their governments peacefully. Islamists eventually abandoned peaceful methods and decided to meet unbending government violence with violence of their own. Islamist extremism, therefore, grew directly out of political repression.

The Process of Radicalization

The journey from political repression to extremism can be viewed in three stages. First, a government hoards resources through corruption, while others suffer in poverty. Then, when groups arise to oppose this injustice, the government denies them a voice in the political process, thereby forcing them to take more extreme measures. Last, members of these opposition groups are jailed, and the jails themselves become breeding grounds for ideological radicalization. "Terrorist movements often arise in reaction to a perceived injustice, as a means to right some terrible wrong, real or imagined,"[9] writes scholar Jessica Stern.

Evidence of this process can be seen in the history of the Muslim Brotherhood. Hassan al-Banna founded the group to oppose government corruption and the unfair treatment of Egypt's workers. "Arabs and Muslims have no status and no dignity,"[10] al-Banna said.

> "Terrorist movements often arise in reaction to a perceived injustice, as a means to right some terrible wrong, real or imagined."[9]
>
> —Jessica Stern, scholar and author

Before the process of radicalization, Muslim Brotherhood members worked for a more just society by setting up night schools to help educate workers and campaigning for more hospitals and doctors. The Muslim Brotherhood also fought for shorter working hours and better pay for Egypt's workers.

Egypt's King Farouk and the governing classes saw this as a direct challenge to their power. They saw the Muslim Brotherhood not as a charity but as a political force that could rally people against the king and threaten the privileges of the rich. Farouk therefore outlawed the Muslim Brotherhood in 1948. As a banned organization, the Muslim Brotherhood, the most popular and widespread organization in Egypt at the time, had to go underground. Members met in secret, often in mosques, trying to elude the king's spies and the police, who would imprison them just for being a member of the group.

A King Is Exiled

Forced into the shadows, members of the Muslim Brotherhood became both more political and more extreme. In their view, Egypt would never be a fair society with Farouk in power. They thus decided to use violence to overthrow the government. This marked a major turning point in the organization's history. The Muslim Brotherhood had adopted direct political goals (the overthrow of the government) and violent methods to achieve those goals.

In 1952 a group of military officers associated with the Muslim Brotherhood deposed Farouk and ordered him into exile. Farouk boarded the royal yacht, but not before he loaded it with crates marked "whisky" and "champagne" that actually contained gold bars from the national treasury. Although the army led the revolt, Farouk bitterly blamed the Muslim Brotherhood. "I admit that I would have enjoyed watching those prudish, clerkly sect-leaders of the Muslim Brotherhood as they drifted through my rooms like elderly ladies on a cook's tour, pulling open drawers, prying into cupboards and wardrobes, and gaping like country bumpkins at the number of the king's clean shirts,"[11] Farouk wrote.

The Brotherhood in Prison

Farouk's corruption had driven the Muslim Brotherhood toward violence. Clashes with Egypt's post-Farouk government completed the process of radicalization. After Farouk's overthrow, a group of army officers, led by Gamal Abdel Nasser, ruled Egypt. They shared the Muslim Brotherhood's disdain for Farouk but had little else in common with the Islamists.

Egypt's military rulers enacted a constitution that adopted Western-style democratic government and limited the role of reli-

Members of a Muslim fundamentalist group await trial in Egypt after a coup attempt in the 1980s. Several attempts have been made over the years to overthrow the country's repressive leaders.

gion in society. Effectively, they adopted the separation of church and state common in the West.

All of this was deeply at odds with the Muslim Brotherhood's goal of returning Egypt to its Islamic traditions. Although the military rulers tolerated the Muslim Brotherhood after Farouk's overthrow, it was an uneasy truce. When in 1956 the Muslim Brotherhood unsuccessfully attempted to assassinate Nasser, he responded by once again outlawing the group and rounding up its members by the thousands.

Prison helped complete the radicalization of this once peaceful Islamist group into an extremist organization that embraced violence and intolerance. In prison, Islamists sought out fellow Islamists and together nursed their grievances against the government. A violent new generation of leaders arose in these prisons, including Sayyid Qutb. "Egypt's brutal prisons hardened Islamists such as Sayed Qutb," notes the *Economist*. "His radical vision fuelled a new generation's darker dreams of jihad, vengeance and martyrdom, not only in Egypt but across the Muslim world."[12]

> "Egypt's brutal prisons hardened Islamists such as Sayed Qutb. His radical vision fuelled a new generation's darker dreams of jihad, vengeance and martyrdom, not only in Egypt but across the Muslim world."[12]
>
> —*The Economist*

Prison radicalization is an ongoing phenomenon, still shaping Islamist terrorists today. Ayman al-Zawahiri, Osama bin Laden's right-hand man and the current leader of al Qaeda, was tortured in Egypt's prisons in the 1980s. "Zawahiri is part of a lineage of giants in the modern jihadi movement who were further radicalized by their years in prison,"[13] notes international relations scholar Brian Till in the *Atlantic*. Political repression and imprisonment were thus major drivers of the growth of Islamist extremism.

Discontent in Iran

This pattern of oppression, imprisonment, and radicalization was repeated in Iran. In the 1960s and 1970s, Iran's ruler, Mohammad Reza Pahlavi, known as the shah, sought to modernize Iran's economy and relied on Western advisors for advice. This reform program, however, was mismanaged. It caused a sharp rise in prices, which made it difficult for the poor to afford food and other basic necessities. "Inflation and other problems spawned by the scope and pace of development created hardships for many Iranians," says Suzanne Maloney of the Brookings Institution. "Economic grievances helped galvanize opposition to the monarchy, and revolutionary leaders such as Ayatollah Ruhollah Khomeini appealed to Iran's poor and its increasingly squeezed middle class."[14]

Opposition to the shah became widespread. Protesters fell into two main groups—the Islamists and the Communists. The shah responded to the calls for political change from both groups with repression. "The crackdown on communists and Islamists—'the red and the black'—in the 1960s and 1970s saw an increasingly authoritarian government clash with dissidents unhappy at western influence in the country, growing state profligacy and low standards of living,"[15] writes journalist and author David Patrikara-kos in *FT Magazine*.

Torture and Triumph in Iran

To crush political opposition, the shah relied on a special police force, the SAVAK. "Under the Shah we could not even think about criticizing the system publicly, because of the Savak,"[16] says shop owner Iraj Nemati.

Those who continued their criticism found themselves in the shah's dungeons, where suspects were regularly tortured. "The victims were first beaten with copper wire whips in the courtyard, then over the months underwent various degrees of torture as they worked their way through the cells in the three-tiered circular prison, leading finally to an appearance before a military tribunal,"[17] notes the *Washington Post*.

Prison and torture only fueled opposition to the widely hated shah. It caused a massive increase in support for the Islamists. In 1979 the shah, fearing for his safety, fled the country, paving the way for the return of Khomeini, who personified the triumph of Islamism. Khomeini established the world's first Islamist-run state, a state born out of the shah's repression.

Having been fully radicalized by the shah's repression and his prisons, the Islamists now in power in Iran exported violence to other Shia communities. "After the 1979 revolution, Iran found receptive adherents among embattled and oppressed Shi'ite groups throughout the Muslim world: many Shi'a found Khomeini's charisma and the stunning success of the Iranian revolution inspiring,"[18] writes Middle East scholar Daniel Byman.

In deeply religious Muslim communities in both Egypt and Iran, despotic governments offended the religious sentiments of their own people and their sense of basic fairness. When people objected, their rulers had them arrested and often tortured, and prisons became the breeding grounds for Islamist extremism. Political repression must therefore be seen as a major driver of the rise of Islamist extremism.

Political Repression Is Not the Main Cause of Islamist Extremism

"There is no standard model of the radicalization process. . . . The process differs by individual, and since there is also no standard profile of the 'typical' radicalized individual, there is no one single model of how individuals radicalize."

—Jennifer Williams, foreign affairs correspondent

Jennifer Williams, "How Ordinary People Decide to Become Terrorists," Vox, November 20, 2015. www.vox.com.

Consider these questions as you read:

1. What did Sayyid Qutb find so disturbing about life in America?
2. Do you think that religion is no longer relevant in the modern world? Why or why not?
3. Why do leaders, like Iran's before and after the revolution, fear people with different political opinions?

Editor's note: The discussion that follows presents common arguments made in support of this perspective. All arguments are supported by facts, quotes, and examples taken from various sources of the period or present day.

If political repression gave rise to Islamist extremism, then it would be logical to assume that in the absence of repression, there would be no extremism. This is simply not the case. While repression was certainly a factor in hardening the beliefs of Islamist extremists, it was not the cause of their beliefs.

History affords us the opportunity to see Islamist extremism during periods when there was no repression. And the conclusion that must be drawn is that Islamist extremism is a potent ideology—one that has existed in periods of political repression and in periods when that repression was absent. Therefore, political repression is not the cause of Islamist extremism.

Qutb in America

It might be useful to ask what Islamists believe in and just why they ended up in the prisons of Egypt and Iran. The case of the Muslim Brotherhood's Sayyid Qutb is particularly instructive. Qutb became a firebrand and the chief advocate for the use of violence to rid Egypt of Western influences and restore Islamic law. But Qutb grew up in a life of privilege, not oppression. He came from a family of landowners who ensured that he got a good education. Qutb became a highly educated literary scholar, and after graduating from college, he took a job with Egypt's Ministry of Education.

He was employed, in other words, by the government that he later tried to overthrow. Nor was his career at the Ministry of Education an unhappy one. The job afforded him status in Egyptian society and opportunities not open to most Egyptians, such as traveling abroad. In 1948 the ministry sent Qutb to the United States to study the US educational system to help modernize Egypt's own universities. He was welcomed by the faculty of the Colorado State College of Education in the town of Greeley, Colorado, for a six-month visit.

Coming from the desert lands of arid Egypt, Qutb remarked on the greenness of the tree-lined streets and grassy lawns of the town. He also found the townspeople pleasant and welcoming. But he saw an emptiness in their lives, as if they were devoid of spiritual purpose. He came to view Americans in general as concerned only with material wealth and enjoyment.

As a deeply conservative Muslim, Qutb was also offended by the sight of male and female students mingling at a church dance, which he thought was highly immoral. Muslim men and women traditionally pray and socialize separately. He saw the more liberal views on women in America as morally corrupting and a threat to tradition. He also saw America's tolerance of different religions— the freedom of religion—as draining religions of their meaning and purpose. "In Qutb's view, this divorce of the secular and the spiritual had inflicted a 'hideous schizophrenia' on modern civilization,"[19] writes journalist Daniel Brogan.

Rejecting the Modern

It was shortly after he returned from America that Qutb joined the Muslim Brotherhood. After diagnosing America as having a spiritual illness, he decided that he must prevent this from infecting Egypt by returning society to the strict doctrines of Islam. America's obsession with material progress, in Qutb's view, could only be countered with a revival of faith that could protect Muslims from the evils of the modern world.

> "Qutb called all true Muslims to jihad, or Holy War, against . . . modernity, which America so powerfully represents."[20]
>
> —David Von Drehle, journalist and author

Moreover, Qutb believed that only violence against non-Muslims and Muslims who disagreed with his strict interpretation of Islam would revive the spiritual life of Muslims. "Qutb called all true Muslims to jihad, or Holy War, against . . . modernity, which America so powerfully represents,"[20] writes journalist David Von Drehle.

Qutb's religious extremism and his advocacy of terrorism thus grew out of his rejection of certain ideas. It was therefore not a reaction to political repression.

Intolerance Grows

If political repression causes the rise of extremism, then that extremism should wane when Islamists are not repressed. History shows that this is not the case. When the Egyptian army overthrew King Farouk, the Muslim Brotherhood was invited to cooperate with the new government. But the organization had become so unbending that it rejected any compromise with the new government.

The Islamists were particularly unbending on the question of the role of religion. When the new government rejected the Islamists' demands to write a constitution based on Islamic teachings, the Muslim Brotherhood took up arms once again. Their extremist ideology—not political repression—drove them back into opposition. "I cannot bow down pleading for mercy before injustice and error,"[21] Qutb replied. His extremist views prevented him from reasonable compromise, and Egypt's government thought it best to execute him. Qutb was hanged in August 1966.

The Brotherhood in Power

Yet history provides an even more convincing example of how in the absence of repression the Muslim Brotherhood reverted to extremist ideology. In 2011 change was sweeping across the Middle East, in a movement known as the Arab Spring. Peaceful protesters took to the streets in various Arab capitals and demanded more say over their own government. In Egypt thirty years of rule by a military dictator named Hosni Mubarak was put to an end, largely peacefully.

As a result, the Muslim Brotherhood was once again legalized as a political party. It changed its name to the Freedom and Justice Party, and its candidate Mohamed Morsi won the presidency in the following year's national election. After more than eighty years, the Muslim Brotherhood found itself in control of Egypt. Morsi became the first Islamist elected as leader of an Arab nation.

Two things happened in short order. The Muslim Brotherhood split between moderates, who worked within the democratic system (headed by Morsi), and hard-liners, who wanted a fully Islamic state and refused to compromise with other political parties. Secondly, Morsi (representing the moderates) tried to write a constitution that represented the values of the Islamists above other groups in society. "Morsi awarded himself total executive control, allowing himself to bypass judicial procedures to ensure the text was put to a public vote without further debate," writes journalist Patrick Kingsley. "The decision led to deadly street fights between

Mohamed Morsi greets supporters at a campaign rally before his 2012 election as Egypt's president. Morsi, who is a member of the Muslim Brotherhood, was the first Islamist to be elected to lead an Arab nation.

Brotherhood supporters and leftists and liberals outside the presidential palace."[22]

In other words, both the hard-liners and the moderates refused to compromise with other groups within Egypt. The Muslim Brotherhood simply could not repress the intolerance of its extremist ideology. In the total absence of repression, and holding complete power, the Islamists sought to further their extremism. Morsi's intolerance, in turn, was met with opposition from the military. The army intervened, overthrew Morsi in 2013, and once again outlawed the Muslim Brotherhood.

Iranian Islamists in Power

The Muslim Brotherhood ruled for only a short period. In Iran, on the other hand, Islamists established a theocratic state that still exists today. One would expect that if political repression under the shah led to Islamist extremism, then extremism would not exist in the absence of the shah's repression. Quite the opposite is true. As soon as Ayatollah Khomeini landed in Tehran, Iran's capital, in 1979, he began to utter anti-Western statements and extremist ideology. The "Great Satan" became the favored term used in Iran for the United States. The Islamic government simply could not tolerate that other countries did not want to adopt their strict view of Islam. "This is not a struggle between the United States and Iran," declared the ayatollah. "This is a struggle between Islam and blasphemy."[23]

Once in power, Iran's Islamists were no more tolerant of political opposition than the shah. Protesters and opposition politicians were once again punished by beatings, torture, and imprisonment. The Islamists also persecuted people whose view of Islam did not agree with their own. In 1988, for example, the ayatollah ordered the death of thousands of political prisoners. Prisoners were asked whether they agreed with the religious policies of the government and whether they were loyal to the Islamists. "If you answered no to any question, they killed you," recalls one prisoner. "I lied to save my life."[24]

> "This is not a struggle between the United States and Iran. This is a struggle between Islam and blasphemy."[23]
>
> —Ayatollah Ruhollah Khomeini, supreme leader of Iran

Decades after the revolution, Iran under the Islamists is no less repressive than Iran was under the shah. "The Iranian government has the highest per capita execution rate in the world, treats women as second class citizens, persecutes gays and religious minorities, and stifles free speech,"[25] writes Karim Sadjadpour, a scholar of Iran.

Prisons may have provided an opportunity for Islamists to spread their ideology and recruit new members for extremist groups. But history shows that Islamist extremism existed in the absence of repression. It also shows that once in power, the Islamists' political and religious ideas—their ideology—prevented them from compromise or moderation. Therefore, it is clear that Islamist extremism did not result from political repression, though it is very likely to cause it.

Chapter Three

Has Western Intervention in the Middle East Caused Islamist Extremism?

Western Intervention in the Middle East Is a Main Driver of Islamist Extremism

- Western backing for dictators in Muslim countries fueled extremism.
- Western support for secular rulers led to the belief that the West wanted to undermine Islam.
- Western military interventions led directly to surges in terrorism.

The Debate at a Glance

Islamist Extremism Is Driven by Ideology, Not by Western Intervention

- Islamist extremists use the West as an excuse to spread their ideology.
- Extremists are most concerned with promoting their version of Islam among other Muslims.
- The majority of victims of Islamist violence are Muslims in the Middle East, not people in the West.

Western Intervention in the Middle East Is a Main Driver of Islamist Extremism

"History takes no prisoners. It shows, with absolute lucidity, that the Islamic extremism ravaging the world today was borne out of the Western foreign policy of yesteryear."

—Ben Norton, journalist

Ben Norton, "We Created Islamic Extremism: Those Blaming Islam for ISIS Would Have Supported Osama bin Laden in the '80s," *Salon*, November 17, 2015. www.salon.com.

Consider these questions as you read:

1. Why do you think Western democracies have supported dictators in the Muslim world?
2. Do you believe that hostility in Iran toward the United States and the United Kingdom is justified? Why or why not?
3. What are some of the reasons that many Muslims were angered by the presence of Western troops defending Arab nations in the Gulf War?

Editor's note: The discussion that follows presents common arguments made in support of this perspective. All arguments are supported by facts, quotes, and examples taken from various sources of the period or present day.

In the history of the rise of Islamist extremism, there is one recurrent theme—opposition to Western interference in Muslim societies. In Egypt, British support for King Farouk led to the founding of the Muslim Brotherhood. In Iran first the British and then the Americans helped prop up royal rulers who enriched themselves while their people lived in poverty. In later years Western governments initially supported dictators like Saddam Hussein in Iraq or Hosni Mubarak in Egypt.

In the minds of Islamists, Western interference became a major cause of the sufferings of Muslims. The injustice inflicted on Muslims by repressive regimes at home could only exist, they believed, because of the guns and money that local leaders got from the West. Al Qaeda's campaign of violence, therefore, was directed both at regional governments that cooperated with the West and at the Western countries that supported them. Khalid Sheikh Mohammed, the mastermind of the 9/11 attacks on the United States, explained his motives in a letter to US president Barack Obama. "It was not we who started the war against you on 9/11," he said. "It was you and your dictators in our land."[26]

> "It was not we who started the war against you on 9/11. It was you and your dictators in our land."[26]
>
> —Khalid Sheikh Mohammed, mastermind of the 9/11 attacks

Islamists have railed against Western interference in the Islamic world, especially the Middle East, in their earliest writings down to their present proclamations. Western interference in these lands was not the sole reason for the rise of Islamist extremism, but it was a major driver of the phenomenon.

Ancient Lands, New Nations

One might ask why Western nations were in the Middle East in the first place. The answer, by and large, is that the colonizing nations sought to gain material or political advantage by controlling other nations. Western nations used their material and military might to lay claim to the lands of other peoples, including most of the Middle East

When the colonial powers, chiefly Great Britain and France, arrived in the Middle East, they found weak governments and stagnant economies. After World War I (1914–1918), the British and the French redrew the map of the Middle East, creating modern countries and expanding their own influence over those countries. "It was immoral, because it decided people's future without asking them,"[27] remarked one Iraqi citizen who rejects the borders of the country she lives in.

The redrawing of national boundaries in the Middle East by colonial powers also challenged a more traditional notion of identity. "In the Western world, the basic unit of human organization is the nation," explains historian Bernard Lewis. "Muslims, however, tend to see not a nation subdivided into religious groups but a religion subdivided into nations. This is no doubt partly because most of the nation-states that make up the modern Middle East are relatively new creations, left over from the era of Anglo-French imperial domination."[28]

A primary motivation in the Islamist struggle is to erase those colonial borders and to reunite all Muslims under Islamic law, known as sharia. The perceived threat to their religion and their political self-determination therefore fueled the Islamist desire to attack the West and rid the Islamic world of Western influence.

Aiding Repression in Iran

Islamism allowed Muslims to conceive of their struggle against the West as a defense of their religion and traditions. Islamists could therefore claim to be defending Islam as a civilization from an alien Christian civilization that arrived with Western interference in their countries.

In the Islamists' view the Western assault on the Islamic world arrived in two forms—support for non-Islamic secular governments and direct military intervention in Muslim countries. The first can be seen in the history of Western involvement in modern Iran. The shah of Iran was a close US ally during World War II (1939–1945), and after the war US support for Iran increased for two reasons. The first was that the US government wanted to prevent Iranian Communists from coming to power and forming a pro-Russian Communist government. Iran was therefore seen as an important US ally in the Cold War—a global political struggle between Western democracies and the Soviet Union that lasted from 1947 to 1991. The second reason was commercial. The US economy relied heavily on oil, and the Americans wanted to ensure continued access to Iran's oil fields.

Opposition groups in Iran resented US support for the shah, who was widely seen as corrupt and a puppet of the West. When the United States undermined the democratically elected government of Mohammad Mosaddegh in 1951, Iranians were further angered. Mosaddegh had promised to end corruption and to use Iran's oil wealth to benefit the general population. He also promised to end British and American control of the Iranian oil industry through a policy known as nationalization—the state takeover of private companies.

> "Ultimately, the United States was blamed for the thousands killed . . . by the Iranian army, which was trained, equipped, and seemingly controlled by Washington."[29]
>
> —Richard Cottam, scholar of US-Iranian relations

This proved to be too much for the British and Americans, who used their intelligence agencies to overthrow Mosaddegh in 1953. He was imprisoned by the shah, and his followers were rounded up, tortured, and in many cases executed. British and American support for the shah convinced many Iranians that the West was the enemy of the Iranian people. "Ultimately, the United States was blamed for the thousands killed . . . by the Iranian army, which was trained, equipped, and seemingly controlled by Washington," Richard Cottam, a scholar of US-Iranian relations, wrote in 1979 in explanation of the causes of the Iranian Revolution. "Virtually every wall in Iran carried a slogan demanding the death of the 'American shah.'"[29]

Western Armies in Islam's Home

By supporting repressive, brutal regimes in the Islamic world, the West gave the Islamists a cause and a focus for their anger. The Islamist argument that the West intended to destroy Islam was further confirmed, in their view, when Western troops arrived in the Middle East to wage war against Muslims.

When the Iraqi dictator Saddam Hussein, for example, invaded Kuwait in 1990, Arab anger was quickly deflected away from his

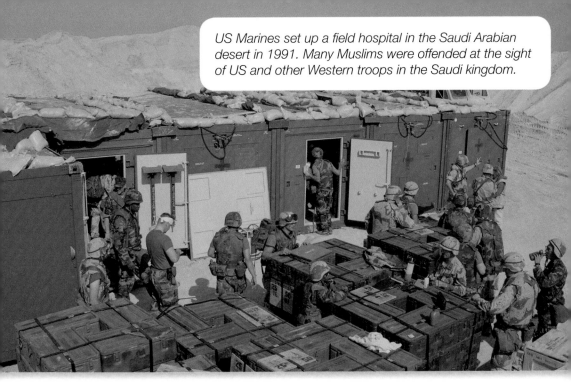

US Marines set up a field hospital in the Saudi Arabian desert in 1991. Many Muslims were offended at the sight of US and other Western troops in the Saudi kingdom.

aggression and toward the US-led military force that was arriving in Saudi Arabia. As the birthplace of Islam, Saudi Arabia is considered by many Muslims to be sacred land. Saudi leaders had asked for Western help because they feared Iraq might attack their kingdom next. Even so, many Muslims were offended by the sight of American and other Western troops rolling through Saudi Arabia like some kind of conquering army. Many Muslims saw the West as a far greater threat to Islam than a squabble between Iraq and its neighbors.

When the US-led coalition of thirty-five countries launched a counterstrike against Iraqi troops, the televised war gave the world a spectacle of terrifying destruction. Allied planes bombed Iraq's capital and Iraqi troop positions in Iraq and Kuwait. Smoldering Iraqi army vehicles littered the roads, which became known as highways of death. In only one hundred hours, the allied ground invasion had shattered the Iraqi army and liberated Kuwait.

Islamists Strike Back

The disparity between the highly sophisticated weapons of the Western-led armies and the poorly armed Iraqi forces reinforced

Islamist propaganda that Muslims were the victims of Western aggression. "The Gulf War," wrote international relations scholar Samuel P. Huntington, "left many [Arabs] feeling humiliated and resentful of the West's military presence in the Persian Gulf, the West's overwhelming military dominance, and their apparent inability to shape their own destiny."[30]

After the war, US troops stayed in Saudi Arabia, which was still fearful of an attack from Iraq. But the Saudis restricted Western troops to isolated areas so as not to advertise their presence. The Islamists initiated a campaign of violence against the US troops anyway. In 1996 Islamists drove a truck bomb into a residential building known as the Khobar Towers, killing twenty-four Americans and wounding nearly five hundred people from various countries. In 2003 suicide bombers struck more residences in the capital, Riyadh, killing thirty-nine and wounding nearly two hundred.

This was the work of al Qaeda, and the motivation of its leader, Osama bin Laden, was the outrage he felt over seeing Western troops in the Muslim holy land. Robert Fisk, a journalist, describes a 1993 interview he conducted in Bin Laden's hideout in Afghanistan. "Determined to overthrow the monarchy in Saudi Arabia and oust the Americans from the Kingdom, [Bin Laden] is describing the bombings that slaughtered 24 Americans in Riyadh and Khobar-Dhahran as a symbol of Saudi anger, the presence of US forces as an 'insult' to the Saudi people,"[31] Fisk writes.

Bin Laden would later mock President George W. Bush for saying that al Qaeda attacked it on September 11, 2001, because the terrorists hated America's freedoms. Bin Laden thought this was nonsense. He argued that 9/11 was punishment for the US troop presence in Saudi Arabia and retribution for the Muslim deaths resulting from Western wars in the Middle East. Bin Laden and others have made it clear that Islamist extremism arose in direct opposition to Western interference. Therefore, it is beyond question that Western intervention in Muslim lands became a major cause of Islamist extremism.

Islamist Extremism Is Driven by Ideology, Not by Western Intervention

"Enough of blaming the West. Isil [the Islamic State terrorist group] has attacked 30 different countries, and the vast majority of its victims in Iraq, Syria, Turkey, Egypt, Saudi Arabia, Pakistan, Bangladesh and elsewhere are Muslims."

—Ed Husain, adjunct senior fellow at the Council on Foreign Relations

Ed Husain, "Enough of Blaming the West. The Terror Will Continue Until Muslims Reject the Need for a Caliphate," *Telegraph* (London), August 18, 2017. www.telegraph.co.uk.

Consider these questions as you read:

1. Why might it be useful for Islamists to blame the West for problems in their own societies?
2. Why do Islamists disapprove of things that are considered normal in the West, like dancing and music?
3. Why do some Muslims who grow up in democratic Western countries turn to extremism?

Editor's note: The discussion that follows presents common arguments made in support of this perspective. All arguments are supported by facts, quotes, and examples taken from various sources of the period or present day.

The argument that Islamist extremism arose in opposition to the West is convenient. It is an easy story to tell in black-and-white terms. When the West arrived in the Middle East with modern weaponry and un-Islamic ideas, the Islamists resisted. Armed only with their Islamic faith and guerrilla warfare tactics, Muslims struck back at the un-Islamic infidels who had meddled in the sacred lands of Islam. Their successes showed that the Islamic world was spiritually powerful despite its material poverty.

The Islamists themselves like this narrative, and they often portray themselves as holy warriors or as paladins—champions of a sacred cause. "The leader of al Qaeda always wanted to be seen, above all else, as the Muslim world's anti-American paladin—fighting the good fight,"[32] writes Reuel Marc Gerecht, an author and former CIA officer.

There is a good deal of fictional romance in the stories that Islamists tell about themselves, and the West features prominently in those stories as the bad guy. This gives the West a place out of proportion to the actual priorities of Islamists. For most of their history, Islamist extremists have spent their efforts trying to reshape their communities in their own image. This means that attentions are focused most of all on their own societies. The actions of the West might anger some in the Middle East, but it is more often an excuse for the violence of extremists, not the cause. The West therefore cannot be seen as a main driver of Islamist extremism.

Enough to Hate at Home

It is worth remembering that while Bin Laden made the United States enemy number one, most Islamists disagreed with him. Their concerns were closer to home. And the focus of their struggle has always been the reshaping of Islamic practice.

Above all, Islamists desire to restore Islam to its roots—its original seventh-century religious traditions. In order to achieve this dream, the Islamists must first convince other Muslims that the Islamists alone understand the correct form of Islam, the true Islam. Rohan Gunaratna, a senior fellow at the Combating Terrorism Center at the US Military Academy at West Point, explains:

Theologically, they legitimate their struggle against fellow Muslims as a struggle between "true Islam" or "pure Islam" and heresy. The former can only be implemented if a true Islamic society and the rule of Sharia can be established. Of course, to achieve this end, Islam will need a militant Islamic movement to provide leadership and spiritual guidance, and to check the threat posed by the global conspiracy that is trying to eradicate Islam by spreading godless and atheistic views among the Muslim masses.[33]

Thus, the first and most important target is not the West but the near enemy—local non-Islamist governments and other Muslims who disagree with their extreme interpretation of Islam. This means that Islamists are at war with everyone who disagrees with them. Islamist extremists, in fact, hate nearly everyone. They hate people who believe in other religions, Muslims of other sects, and Muslims of the same sect who reject their extremism. They hate nonbelievers, and they hate people who believe that religions can coexist peacefully.

Islamist extremists also hate certain behaviors. They hate drinking, which is forbidden to all Muslims, and smoking. They hate music and dancing. They hate women who question the authority of men and sons who disobey their fathers. Islamists offer non-Islamists of all sorts a stark choice—believe what I believe or you are my enemy.

> "Theologically, they legitimate their struggle against fellow Muslims as a struggle between 'true Islam' or 'pure Islam' and heresy."[33]
>
> —Rohan Gunaratna, senior fellow at the US Military Academy's Combating Terrorism Center

Hate in Action

That unrelenting hatred has led to a violent jihad, purportedly to cleanse the Islamic community. This campaign has caused the deaths of many Muslims. Americans can be forgiven for paying more attention to the devastating events of 9/11, and the British can be forgiven for paying more attention to a subway bombing in London. But this obscures the fact that most victims of Islamist extremism are Muslim, and most of those victims live in the Middle East.

Those victims, moreover, often have nothing to do with any particular government or political party. They are simply victims of the terrorists' indiscriminate killing. How can it be that Islamists claim to be fighting a justified war against the West to protect the Muslim community when they are killing innocent Muslims? According to the Koran, Muslims are permitted to defend their community only when it is being persecuted. Otherwise, killing is forbidden. Islamist extremists use this as a justification for their campaigns of terror and violence against the West. But they have no justification for the killing of fellow Muslims, who account for the majority of the victims of their violence. "This is important for a few reasons," writes national security correspondent Eli Lake. "To start it puts the lie to the mantra of the Islamic State, al Qaeda and other Islamic terrorists that they are protecting the faith from the West. These groups are

The city of Mosul in Iraq lies in ruins after years of occupation by Islamist extremists. Although extremists have attacked the West, the vast majority of their victims have been other Muslims in the Middle East.

responsible for turning their battlefields into abattoirs [slaughter-houses]. They slaughter the group they claim to protect."[34]

The claim by Islamist extremists that they are the defenders of Islam is also undercut by their lack of support among the Muslims they claim to represent. The Pew Research Center, which regularly surveys attitudes in the Islamic world, found that in 2013 only 13 percent of Muslims in the countries surveyed had a favorable view of al Qaeda, while 57 percent had an unfavorable view. "Support for al Qaeda, the terrorist organization that bin Laden founded, was low among the Muslim publics surveyed when we first asked the question in 2010, and remained low in 2013, two years after bin Laden's ignominious end,"[35] writes Jacob Poushter of the Pew Research Center.

Muslims in the West

The idea that Islamist extremism arose in opposition to the West is also undercut by the peaceful coexistence of Muslims and non-Muslims in the same Western countries that are seen by Islamists as the enemy. Muslim immigrants represent the fastest-growing segments of the populations of many Western nations. The overwhelming majority live in peace with non-Muslims in their adopted countries.

While Islamist extremists rail against the West, many ordinary Muslims choose to move to Europe and North America to escape the violence and hatred of the extremists—and to practice their religion in peace.

Ideology, however, knows no borders. It follows Muslims through word of mouth and through publications and the Internet. This has resulted in a tiny fraction of Muslims in the West also being seduced by Islamist extremism. Ed Husain, a Muslim who grew up in Great Britain, was swayed by the ideology of the Islamists for a time before he renounced it. His experience shows the power of Islamist ideology even among people who have never lived in the Middle East. Husain points out that he and other Islamists living in

Britain were "fully Western and fully Muslim, free from the political burdens of the Arab world."[36]

Many have pointed out that if it is the ideology of Islamism that creates extremism, then ideas must be used to counter it. In this point of view, it is the West's tolerance for different religions, lifestyles, and peoples that provides an antidote to the intolerance of Islamist extremism.

> "British foreign policy is not the problem; it is part of the solution."[37]
>
> —Boris Johnson, British foreign secretary

Great Britain's foreign secretary, Boris Johnson, is a proponent of this point of view. While he concedes that the West has created resentment because of its past military adventures in the Middle East, he argues that the ideas of the West, namely religious tolerance and democracy, provide an antidote to extremism. Says Johnson:

> British foreign policy is not the problem; it is part of the solution. Above all, we will win when we understand that "we" means not just us in the west, but the hundreds of millions of Muslims around the world who share the same hopes and dreams, who have the same anxieties and goals for their families, who are equally engaged with the world and all its excitements and possibilities, who are equally determined to beat this plague.[37]

Whether Johnson is right is an open question. But both Husain and Johnson, who grew up in the same country, agree that dislike of the foreign policy is not the underlying cause of Islamist radicalization. The real culprit is the intolerant ideology that leads extremists toward violence. Extremist ideology, therefore, is considerably more important in explaining the rise of Islamist extremism than Western interference in the Muslim world.

Chapter Four

Does Poverty Cause Islamist Extremism?

Poverty Is a Major Driver of Islamist Extremism

- Poverty makes people more receptive to extremist ideology.
- A lack of job opportunities makes it more likely that young men will become extremists.
- Terrorists often recruit from among the poor by offering wages or other benefits.

The Debate at a Glance

Poverty Is Not a Major Cause of Islamist Extremism

- Academic research has shown that there is no causal link between poverty and extremism.
- Terrorists are often better educated with more opportunities than their fellow citizens.
- Radicalization, political anger, and personal experiences drive extremism.

Poverty Is a Major Driver of Islamist Extremism

"We have a huge common interest in dealing with this issue of poverty, which in many cases is the root cause of terrorism."

—John Kerry, former US secretary of state

Quoted in David Sterman, "Don't Dismiss Poverty's Role in Terrorism Yet," *Time*, February 4, 2015. www.time.com.

Consider these questions as you read:

1. Why might people living in poverty be attracted to extremist views?
2. Which do you think plays a bigger role in the rise of Islamist extremism: poverty or ideology? Explain your answer.
3. Should richer countries help eradicate poverty in poorer countries? Are there benefits to this approach even to the countries providing assistance? Explain.

Editor's note: The discussion that follows presents common arguments made in support of this perspective. All arguments are supported by facts, quotes, and examples taken from various sources of the period or present day.

Why do some people become violent extremists and others do not? Academics who study the underlying conditions that make extremism more likely cite one factor in particular: poverty. To understand the link between poverty and terrorism, we must understand how poverty limits opportunity, limits education, and leads to desperation. Researchers have found good evidence of a causal relationship between poverty and terrorism, but that relationship is complicated and not always direct. It is nonetheless a key factor in understanding the rise of extreme Islamist ideology. Colin Powell, who spent most of his career in the US military before serving as US secretary of state, came to just this conclusion after grappling with the problem of terrorism for many years. "We can't just stop with a single terrorist or terrorist organization," Powell says. "We have to go and root out the whole system. We have to go after poverty."[38]

Who Is at Risk?

The Muslim world is vast and varied in terms of wealth. There are oil-rich states that have a higher annual income per person than the United States. There are also desperately poor people living in or near these countries. A 2017 study by the United Nations Children's Emergency Fund (UNICEF) studied poverty in eleven countries in the Middle East and North Africa and found that one in four children in the region live in poverty, some 29 million children in total. "These children are deprived of the minimum requirements in two or more of the most basic life necessities including basic education, decent housing, nutritious food, quality health care, safe water, sanitation and access to information,"[39] UNICEF reports.

People living in extreme poverty in these regions will not necessarily become religious extremists. But research shows that they are more likely to turn to extremism than people who are not affected by poverty. This works in a few different ways. First, poverty reduces access to education. When government schools or nonreligious private schools are absent, religious education often fills the void. Some of these religious schools instruct students in extremist ideology. As a result, students are radicalized at an early age.

Radicalization and the Lack of Opportunity

The FATA Research Centre conducts research on Pakistan's Federally Administered Tribal Areas (FATA), an impoverished region where Islamist extremism is common. A 2012 FATA Research Centre report on extremism and radicalization found that in deeply conservative religious communities, a lack of educational opportunity led to extremism. "Much of the driving force for militancy comes from the low level of secular education available, combined with an extremely religious and conservative culture," the report concludes. "The militant narrative that extremist clergy preach has a special hold on youths and the undereducated."[40]

This brings us to the second way that poverty leads to radicalization. When adults fail to find employment that allows them to support their families, they are more likely to be drawn into religious extremism. This is because religious extremism gives them a rationale for their anger and resentment and a sense of purpose in their lives. Islamists turn the anger of the downtrodden into an ideology of hate.

Unemployment also leads people to make desperate decisions, such as joining militant groups. The Brookings Institution, a nonprofit research group located in Washington, DC, conducted a study in 2017 of the link between unemployment and radicalization and violent extremism in the Middle East and North Africa. The institution concluded that unemployment played a major part in radicalization: "Our results show that relative deprivation has a significant association with radicalization. Individuals with secondary educations who are unemployed or underemployed have the highest risk of becoming radicalized."[41]

Poverty Trumps Religion

In the North African nation of Tunisia, poverty seems to be a major contributing factor to the rise of extremism. It is an interesting test case because there are moderate Islamists in Tunisia, as well as extremists who promote violent jihad. Islamist parties, in fact, hold seats in the Tunisian parliament, where they coexist peacefully with politicians who hold very different views. In fact, a major factor that makes these Islamists moderates is that they do not require everyone else to agree with them. They accept that people can hold different points of view. But Tunisia is also home to extremist groups that use violence against both Tunisians and foreigners in Tunisia in the name of Islam, including shootings at an art museum and at tourist hotels and beaches.

So what determines whether a Tunisian Islamist will become a moderate or an extremist? At a political conference in 2015, Rachid Ghannouchi, the head of the main moderate Islamist party and a respected politician, blamed terrorism and extremism on two factors—poverty and the misinterpretation of Islam. Radicalization, he argued, could not be fought without addressing poverty. "Terrorism is very strongly related to economic crisis," Ghannouchi says. "Many of the people who took the road of extremism are raised in marginalized and poor areas."[42]

> "Many of the people who took the road of extremism are raised in marginalized and poor areas."[42]
>
> —Rachid Ghannouchi, Tunisian politician

Lack of Opportunity in Minnesota

This causal link between poverty and terrorism is also evident in Muslim communities outside the Middle East. Because Islamist extremists recruit soldiers for their jihads through the Internet, extremists have recruited from Muslim communities all over the world. In the United States they were especially successful at recruiting fighters from Minnesota's Somali community, 82 percent of whom live below the poverty line, according to a 2008 US Census Bureau report.

It turns out that poverty among the young, mostly male members of the Somali community led to desperation and hopelessness. Young men who could not find jobs or meaningful roles in their adopted society became prime targets for radicalization. Fartun Weli, who heads a nonprofit organization that helps Somali women in Minnesota, explains the phenomenon to the Voice of America, a US government-funded news source that broadcasts globally: "Kids are being recruited. Yes, this is a fact. What are we going to do about it? We have to talk about the root causes that make Somali kids vulnerable . . . how do we fight poverty, bad school systems, the lack of opportunities. The one thing we need to do is . . . make sure there are opportunities created for our community to exit poverty."[43]

Wages of Terror

There is yet another way extremists take advantage of poverty to swell their ranks—they pay people to join them. Many people who are active in extremist movements strongly believe in the ideas they espouse and are even willing to sacrifice themselves for their cause. But this is not always the case. Many extremist organizations recruit new members among very poor communities. The draw is sometimes money. Other times they offer food and education for the children of recruits in exchange for service to the organization. That service may be nothing more than showing up at protest rallies, but it sometimes involves committing acts of terrorism. For someone who has little money, not much opportunity to earn a living, and no real way to support a family, offers like these can be very enticing.

> "It is love that compels a father to say yes to an extremist who shows up at his hut, promising food and education for his children."[44]
>
> —Jake Harriman, former US soldier turned aid worker

Jake Harriman, a former US soldier turned aid worker, explained this recruitment method and its appeal to those who are unemployed and desperately poor. "Most of the time people commit these [terrorist] acts not out of some misplaced hatred of the West, but out of love for their five-year-old son and three-year-old daughter at home who are starving to death," Harriman writes. "It is love that compels a father to say yes to an extremist who shows up at his hut, promising food and education for his children."[44]

Terrorist organizations like the Islamic State in Iraq and Syria (ISIS) specifically target Muslims who are struggling to survive or have found themselves in desperate situations. In 2016 and 2017,

A resident of a Cairo-area slum hangs her family's clothing so it will dry. Some experts say that people who are severely impoverished are more likely to turn to extremism than people who do not live in poverty.

for example, child refugees fleeing from the violence of civil war in Syria and other military campaigns became prime recruiting targets for ISIS, which needed recruits to replace fighters killed on the battlefield. ISIS preyed on their desperation and displacement. "Young unaccompanied refugees are more vulnerable to radicalisation if they are separated from their parents,"[45] according to a report from the London-based anti-extremism organization the Quilliam Foundation.

The more insecure people are economically, the more susceptible they are to radicalization by extremists. Evidence shows that while poverty and economic instability are not the only causes of extremism, they are quite often major contributing factors.

Poverty Is Not a Major Cause of Islamist Extremism

"Poverty alone does not cause a person to become a terrorist, any more than poverty alone causes somebody to become a criminal."

—Barack Obama, forty-fourth US president

Quoted in Beenish Ahmed, "What's the Real Root Cause of Terrorism: Poverty or Anger?," Think-Progress, February 19, 2015. https://thinkprogress.org.

Consider these questions as you read:

1. Why do you think terrorist leaders tend to come from better-educated, richer families?
2. In your opinion, do Muslims raised in Western countries become extremists because they feel caught between two cultures or because they are exposed to extremist ideas? Explain your answer.
3. Do you think religion and the modern world are incompatible? Why or why not?

Editor's note: The discussion that follows presents common arguments made in support of this perspective. All arguments are supported by facts, quotes, and examples taken from various sources of the period or present day.

The link between poverty and extremism has been much studied by academics. In part this is because if poverty causes extremism, then extremism could theoretically be stopped by ending poverty. This school of thought that sees poverty as a cause of extremism has one major flaw: There is no evidence to support this link.

A 2006 study on terrorism in ninety-six countries between 1986 and 2002 found no causation at all between poverty and terrorism. The study looked at a number of economic factors, such as income, access to food, and unemployment, to see whether there was a connection to extremism or violence. *"None* of the economic indicators are significant predictors of either terrorist incidents or casualties, contrary to the expectations necessary to validate the 'rooted-in-poverty' hypothesis,"[46] writes James A. Piazza, a political scientist and the author of the study.

Thorough academic research on the relationship between poverty and terrorism has consistently shown similar findings. These studies make it clear that poverty is not a major cause of Islamist extremism or terrorism.

Neither Poor nor Less Educated

The premise that poverty contributes to terrorism assumes two things. First, it assumes that poverty leads to desperation, which makes people more likely to lash out at society through violent acts. Second, it assumes that the lack of education that often accompanies poverty leads people to be more easily radicalized and drawn into the world of the extremists. While this argument is logical, it is not supported by fact.

People who carry out violent acts in the name of Islamist extremism, it turns out, are not poorer than other people in their societies. In fact, Islamist extremists tend to be both wealthier and better educated than their peers. This is the case for both the leaders of Islamist organizations and the foot soldiers who carry out terrorist attacks.

Hassan al-Banna, the founder of the Muslim Brotherhood, was a well-educated member of a well-respected family. Al Qaeda's top leaders hailed from even more elite families. The Bin Laden family earned a fortune in the construction industry in Saudi Arabia. Osama bin Laden and his siblings grew up in an environment of wealth, often traveling and studying abroad. Ayman al-Zawahiri, who became the leader of al Qaeda after Bin Laden was killed, was also from a prestigious family of scholars. He was trained as a surgeon and had a bright future in Egypt.

Poverty was clearly not a motivating factor for al Qaeda's leadership. The group's brand of extremism was motivated by politics, not personal circumstances. Referring to al-Zawahiri and Bin Laden, journalist Lawrence Wright states, "They were both members of the educated classes, intensely pious, quiet-spoken, and politically stifled by the regimes in their own countries."[47]

Culture Conflict

Some of the most famous leaders of the Islamist movements came into contact with the West or Westerners largely because of their family's wealth and the opportunities that wealth afforded them. Being educated in Western universities exposed them to people and ideas from around the world. Through that contact they came to see the Western world as incompatible with the strict form of Islam that gave purpose and order to their lives.

The same is true of the less well-known terrorists who carried out the attacks that the leaders of al Qaeda had inspired and en-

A wounded boy is carried to a hospital after a suicide bombing outside a stadium in Afghanistan. People who support, plan, and carry out terrorist attacks are often well-educated and well-off.

couraged. In 2010 Faisal Shahzad, a Pakistani American, attempted to detonate a car bomb in Times Square, a crowded tourist area of New York City. Shahzad's father was a high-ranking member of Pakistan's air force who sent his son to study in the United States. In America, Shahzad went to college, earned a master's degree in business administration, and found a well-paying job.

While this seems like the American dream come true, it turned out that Shahzad also had a secret life. In his quiet hours at home, he was being radicalized by Islamist propaganda through the Internet. He became angrier and angrier about the plight of Muslims subjected to Western military campaigns. He eventually traveled to a terrorist training camp in Pakistan, where he learned to make bombs. On May 1, 2010, he set his plot in motion. It was foiled by a local street vendor who spotted smoke coming from the vehicle. The bomb was defused, and Shahzad was sent to prison for life.

> "The young man who would do his best to secure an American education before succumbing to the call of the jihad is a man in the grip of a deep schizophrenia."[48]
>
> —Fouad Ajami, Middle East scholar

As with so many other terrorists, poverty played no role in Shahzad's radicalization. Like many other Islamist extremists, he was well educated and had employable skills. Fouad Ajami, a scholar of the Middle East, turned to psychology to explain why Shahzad and other Muslims in the West became radicalized. Ajami argues that they are unable to find an identity in the modern world while still safeguarding their traditional identities as Muslims. He describes them as "nowhere men," trapped in a state of psychological confusion, neither Western nor Muslim. "The young man who would do his best to secure an American education before succumbing to the call of the jihad is a man in the grip of a deep schizophrenia," Ajami wrote. "Modernity both attracts and unsettles them. America is at once the object of their dreams and the scapegoat onto which they project their deepest malignancies."[48]

Education and Ideology

The thesis that poverty leads to extremism is also undercut by one of its chief assumptions—namely, that the lack of education among the poor makes them susceptible to radicalization. Researchers have actually discovered the opposite: that terrorism attracts more-educated people. A 2009 study by sociologist Diego Gambetta and political scientist Steffen Hertog found that many Islamic militants had received college degrees and many had also attended graduate school. In their educations, one academic discipline was more commonly studied than others—engineering.

The authors of the study found a high percentage of engineers among the ranks of the extremist groups they studied—nearly a fifth of all extremists—and almost half of all extremists held advanced degrees. The link between engineering and extremism is not clear. "The engineer mind-set, Gambetta and Hertog suggest, might be a mix of emotional conservative and intellectual habits that prefers clear answers to ambiguous questions,"[49] journalist David Berreby writes. In other words, the engineers are well-educated people who are in search of some way to make sense of the world around them. They are a bit like Ajami's "nowhere men," living in a confusing world in which their craving for traditional community exists uneasily with their scientific studies.

The research also suggests a conclusion at odds with the theory that poverty leads to extremism. It suggests that the well-educated and well-off are more likely to be radicalized than people who have little education and live in poverty because the former are more likely to encounter people who espouse radical ideas. "What might explain why so many relatively well-off people from relatively well-off countries end up as terrorists?" the *Economist* asks. "It may be that a certain level of education makes it more likely that people will become politicised."[50]

Terrorists Not for Hire

Researchers have also discovered another interesting factor that undercuts the idea that extremists are created by financial incentives. Research on the motivation for suicide bombings, for example, found no correlation between financial incentives and bombings. Terrorist organizations often pay the families of suicide bombers after the bomber carries out an act of terrorism. An increase in the reward for the family showed no increase in the number of people willing to become suicide bombers. In fact, people who elected to become suicide bombers were ideologically motivated. Money for their families was not an incentive. "The stereotype of suicide bombers being drawn from the ranks of those who are so impoverished that they have nothing to live for may be wildly incorrect,"[51] write Alan B. Krueger and Jitka Malecková, academics who research terrorism and its causes.

> "Most terrorists are not so desperately poor that they have nothing to live for. Instead, they are people who care so fervently about a cause that they are willing to die for it."[52]
>
> —Alan B. Krueger, professor of economics

The body of academic research undercuts the idea that poverty and extremism are connected. Economic desperation and lack of opportunity are not the driving factors in the rise of Islamist extremism. In fact, the opposite is true. It is the ideas spread by Islamist extremists that inspire the radical jihadist struggle. "Most terrorists are not so desperately poor that they have nothing to live for," Krueger writes. "Instead, they are people who care so fervently about a cause that they are willing to die for it."[52]

Chapter Five

Has the War on Terror Been Successful?

The War on Terror Has Largely Been Successful

- The United States has captured or killed those responsible for the 9/11 attacks.
- Major terrorist organizations have been defeated or severely weakened.
- The international community has gotten better at fighting terrorists.

The Debate at a Glance

The War on Terror Has Not Been Successful

- The war on terror relies too heavily on military action and fails to address ideology.
- The number of terrorists has increased dramatically since the war began.
- Extremist ideology spread online has resulted in the new threat of lone wolf terrorism.

The War on Terror Has Largely Been Successful

"[The War on Terror] was an unconventional war by an unconventional enemy embedded within a worldwide religious community. Yet in a decade, we largely disarmed and defeated it."

—Charles Krauthammer, columnist

Charles Krauthammer, "The War on Terror Has Been a Success," *Los Angeles Daily News*, September 9, 2011. www.dailynews.com.

Consider these questions as you read:

1. Do you believe the global war on terror can be won by military means alone? Why or why not?
2. Since the Taliban were harboring al Qaeda, did a US-led coalition have the right to invade even though Afghanistan is a sovereign nation? Explain your answer.
3. How do you imagine the war on terror ending? Will it ever end? Explain.

Editor's note: The discussion that follows presents common arguments made in support of this perspective. All arguments are supported by facts, quotes, and examples taken from various sources of the period or present day.

The terrorist attacks on the United States on September 11, 2001, provoked a reaction that is still playing out today. This is the global war on terror. Weighing the success of this military campaign requires answering a few central questions. Were the perpetrators of 9/11 hunted down and brought to justice? Has the United States prevented another 9/11? Is there global cooperation for combating terrorism? Are the terrorists on the run? Events since 2001 indicate that the answer to all these questions is yes. Therefore, the global war on terror must be considered a success, even though terrorism has not been totally eradicated and the war is far from over. "There have been no more 9/11s, none of the worst cases that post-9/11 extrapolations suggested," writes Brian Michael Jenkins of the Rand Corporation, a think tank. "The 9/11 attacks now appear to be a statistical outlier, not a forerunner of further escalation."[53]

Putting Terrorists on the Run

When President George W. Bush declared on September 20, 2001, a new type of war against a stateless enemy, it was unclear whether America's allies would respond to the call. Bush's first major success in the war on terror was therefore gaining the support of America's allies in Europe. Throughout the Cold War, Europe and America had hammered out a defense treaty to protect Europe from Soviet invasion. This was the North Atlantic Treaty Organization (NATO). At the core of the treaty is Article 5, which requires all members to come to the defense of any member that is attacked. For the entirety of the Cold War, this article went unused. The first and only time it has been triggered was in response to 9/11. By triggering Article 5, Europe was signaling that it would support the United States as an active partner in the global war on terror. "NATO also made clear for the first time that it was prepared to see some acts of terrorism as acts of war, even if such circumstances were not envisioned when the treaty was written in 1949,"[54] writes Suzanne Daley in the New York Times.

This first hurdle in launching the war on terror had been overcome. American would not go to war alone. On October 7, 2001, when bombs began targeting Islamist extremists in Afghanistan, US forces were joined by the British military, and dozens of nations contributed troops in the months that followed.

Decimating Al Qaeda

This US coalition then went to war to destroy al Qaeda in its bases in Afghanistan. Because the government of Afghanistan was controlled by religious fundamentalists known as the Taliban, success in the military campaign would be determined by the coalition's ability to overcome the Taliban forces and destroy al Qaeda's terrorist camps. Despite the overwhelming technical superiority of the militaries of the invading nations, success would depend on convincing tribes in Afghanistan to rise up against the Taliban. An insurgent army known as the Northern Alliance was already fighting the Taliban, and this army acted as the major ground force once the US-led invasion of Afghanistan began.

Less than three months later, the combination of Northern Alliance fighters on foot or horseback combined with British and American special operations forces and massive air power had driven the Taliban from power and robbed al Qaeda of its

Citizens of Kabul in Afghanistan greet triumphant Northern Alliance soldiers after the Taliban fled the city in 2001. The defeat of the Taliban marked an important victory against Islamist extremists.

training camps. Michael E. O'Hanlon, a senior fellow in foreign policy at the Brookings Institution, describes the rapid success of this opening battle in the global war on terror. "Beginning on October 7, Afghans, Americans, and coalition partners cooperated to produce a remarkable military victory in Afghanistan," he writes. "Together they defeated the Taliban forces, estimated at 50,000 to 60,000 strong, as well as a few thousand al Qaeda fighters."[55]

The victory was swift but not complete. As the remaining al Qaeda fighters slowed advancing US and Northern Alliance forces, al Qaeda's leadership slipped out of Afghanistan into Pakistan. This opened an entirely new phase of a secret war against terrorism that stretched around the globe. Success in the war on terror would ultimately be determined by the fate of Osama bin Laden and al Qaeda's other leaders.

Capture or Kill

The CIA set up special units to track major terrorist figures and worked closely with the FBI and intelligence and law enforcement partners overseas. It was a cat-and-mouse game combining sophisticated Western intelligence information gleaned from satellites and cell phones with the local knowledge of intelligence agents on the ground.

In the search for al Qaeda's operational commander, Khalid Sheikh Mohammed, for example, a joint team of US agents and Pakistani intelligence officers followed a lead to Karachi, Pakistan. "The soldiers moved in at sunrise and all hell broke loose," write Terry McDermott and Josh Myer in the *Atlantic*. "Hundreds of rounds, hours of shooting and grenade throwing, and two dead men later, the authorities secured the building."[56]

Mohammed had escaped, but the information found during the raid led to his capture on March 1, 2003, when he was cornered in another city in Pakistan. In the years after 9/11, al

Qaeda's leadership was systematically captured or killed in thousands of similar raids. The war on terror reached a crucial moment on May 2, 2011, when US forces killed Osama bin Laden in a raid on a compound in Abbottabad, Pakistan. "Today, al Qaeda is on its heels and Osama bin Laden is no more,"[57] proclaimed US president Barack Obama.

> "Today, al Qaeda is on its heels and Osama bin Laden is no more."[57]
>
> —US president Barack Obama

The Learning Curve

Although al Qaeda has been much weakened by the global war on terror, terrorism has evolved. The success of the war on terror in degrading al Qaeda and killing or capturing its leaders is indisputable. But the terrorist threat has continued to evolve, and new terrorist threats have emerged. Determining the success of the war on terror requires an assessment of how the global community has responded to these new threats.

The most violent terrorist group to arise since al Qaeda was ISIS. In containing the rise of this budding terrorist state and ultimately destroying it, the international community demonstrated that it had learned many lessons in the war on terror. When ISIS proclaimed the creation of the Islamic State in parts of Iraq and Syria, this terrorist entity threatened not just Iraq and Syria but all the countries in the region. Western nations responded with coalition building, training local troops, and using special forces and air power. This new front in the global war on terror provided a major test of international cooperation and coalition building.

Iraqi Kurds, Sunni Iraqi Arabs, Shia Iraqi militias, Syrian Kurds, and Turks all attacked ISIS from various sides, while US, French, British, and other Western militaries provided air support, intelligence, and special forces soldiers. In total, twenty-three countries contributed to the effort to destroy ISIS. Western troops kept a low profile, so as not to anger local populations by their presence. It was a marked departure from the many mistakes made by the United States during the Iraq War, when US bombing missions often enflamed public opinion, especially when they missed their targets and killed civilians. The combatants in the global war on terror had gotten smarter, and by late 2017 ISIS had been entirely driven from Iraq and operated only in isolated pockets in Syria. "Our heroic armed forces have now secured the entire length of the Iraq-Syria border," Iraqi prime minister Haider al-Abadi said in December 2017. "We defeated Daesh [ISIS] through our unity and sacrifice for the nation."[58]

In 2011, on the tenth anniversary of 9/11, the US intelligence community released an overview of the war on terror in the *National Strategy for Counterterrorism*. The report reads:

> In the decade since the September 11 attacks, we as a government have become much more effective in executing our CT [counterterrorism] mission—with a critical measure of this success reflected in the broad array of countries and capabilities that are now arrayed in the fight against al-Qa'ida. Indeed, nobody is more aware of our increased effectiveness than al-Qa'ida and its affiliates and adherents, as their plans are disrupted, their capabilities degraded, and their organizations dismantled.[59]

In the years since 9/11, al Qaeda, the Taliban, and ISIS have all seen their power sharply reduced and thousands of their members killed or captured. The perpetrators of 9/11 have also been eliminated, and as al Qaeda lingers, its members mostly remain in hiding for fear of being targeted by international efforts. The global coalition that emerged out of the war on terror is now highly effective at countering new terrorist threats. It can be concluded, therefore, that the war on terror has largely been a success.

The War on Terror Has Not Been Successful

"Seldom has a war been so comprehensively and visibly lost as 'the war on terror' and it is doing a favour to Isis and al-Qaeda not to recognise this and try for something better."

—Patrick Cockburn, Middle East correspondent for the UK newspaper the *Independent*

Patrick Cockburn, "The Government Has Known Since 2003 That the Failed 'War on Terror' Could Cause an Attack like the One in Manchester," *Independent* (London), May 26, 2017. www.independent.co.uk.

Consider these questions as you read:

1. If the Internet is used for online recruitment by extremists, should it be policed and have content blocked or removed? Why or why not?
2. What role does prejudice against Muslims in the United States and Europe play in Islamist radicalization?
3. Why might people living in the West be more attracted to the ideas of Islamist extremism than the ideas of the societies they live in?

Editor's note: The discussion that follows presents common arguments made in support of this perspective. All arguments are supported by facts, quotes, and examples taken from various sources of the period or present day.

The war on terror is based on a conceptual flaw. It assumes that Islamist ideology can be defeated through military action. It is a military response, in other words, to a problem that spreads through ideas. Terrorist leaders have been apprehended or killed by special forces or drone strikes. The Islamic State, which attempted to create an actual country governed by extremist ideology, has been destroyed because it occupied territory that could be attacked by the aircraft, artillery, and ground forces of much more modern militaries.

Yet none of these battlefield successes has reduced the number of terrorists or the threat of terrorism. "A strategy based on invading or bombing might make sense if the number of militants were finite," writes journalist and author Stephen Kinzer. "It is not. Terror groups in the Middle East are attracting recruits faster than they can process them. Killing some creates more, not fewer."[60]

Extremist ideology has attracted an ever-larger number of people since the war on terror was launched in 2001. The war on terror therefore must be seen as ill-conceived and ineffective.

Terror by the Numbers

Graeme Wood, a journalist and author, points to two numbers that indicate what has happened with terrorism since 9/11: 400 and 40,000. The first is roughly the number of al Qaeda members on September 11, 2001. The second is the number of Islamist radicals who flocked to join ISIS fifteen years later. "The challenge for today's terrorism experts is to explain how 400 grew into more than 40,000, despite the combined counterterrorism efforts of dozens of countries,"[61] Wood writes.

And that is not even the full extent of terrorism's spread in the years since 9/11. A study by the Costs of War Project at Brown University shows that the war on terror has spread from Afghanistan, where it began, to seventy-six countries, about 39 percent of the total number of countries in the world. This figure includes countries in which military force is directly used by the coalition fighting global terror, such as Afghanistan, Iraq, and Syria. It also includes countries where the US military strikes terrorists with drones—places like Somalia, Yemen, and Pakistan. And it includes places where the US military or other forces are conducting special operations raids on terrorist targets on their own or in conjunction with local forces.

Journalist Tom Engelhardt, who has written about the sprawling nature of the war, contends that it has failed in its singular purpose—ending Islamist extremism—and created a more dangerous and unstable world. He notes that the war on terror began with fighting in just one country. "Now, the count is 76 and rising," he writes. "Meanwhile, great cities have been turned into rubble; tens of millions of human beings have been displaced from their homes; refugees by the millions continue to cross borders, unsettling ever more lands; terror groups have become brand names across significant parts of the planet."[62]

A Truly Global Fight

US troops are not alone in conducting the war on terror. This war is taking place in countries all around the globe. In the Philippines, the government is fighting an Islamist insurgency. Indonesia has experienced a spate of terrorist attacks. In almost every country in the Middle East, there are now counterterrorism operations conducted by local governments. Africa has become a major new

Indonesian special forces soldiers storm a building during an counterterrorism drill. Since the start of the War on Terror, countries around the world have been forced to prepare for and grapple with violence by Islamist extremists.

battlefield. Some African governments have even invited troops from former colonial powers back to the region to help combat armed Islamist groups.

In February 2018, for example, French fighter jets killed ten extremist fighters in the West African country of Mali, a former French colony. "The offensive was part of France's Operation Barkhane, active in Mali as well as four other former French colonies in West Africa—Mauritania, Niger, Chad and Burkina Faso," reports Agence France-Presse, a French news agency. "These countries form the so-called G5 Sahel, a French-supported group that launched a joint military force to combat extremist organisations last year."[63]

After seventeen years of expansion, the war on terror is so extensive that even the governments sending troops into combat do not always know where they are. When Islamist militants ambushed four US soldiers in the West African nation of Niger in October 2017, US senators admitted they had no idea there were US forces operating in West Africa. "I didn't know there was 1,000 troops in Niger," Senator Lindsey Graham said on NBC's *Meet the Press*, despite the fact that he sits on the Senate's Armed Services Committee, which conducts oversight of US military operations. "This is an endless war without boundaries and no limitation on time and geography."[64]

> "This is an endless war without boundaries and no limitation on time and geography."[64]
>
> —Lindsey Graham, US senator

War Begets Terror

One of the reasons for the failure of the war on terror is the assumption that violence is the answer to extremist ideology. Indeed, no sooner had the dust settled in Afghanistan than al Qaeda began to spread its ideology through propaganda.

This was especially true when the United States and its Allies invaded Iraq in 2003. Al Qaeda used TV footage of bombs

falling on Iraqi villages and terrifying nighttime bombings to anger
Muslims. The many civilian deaths
caused by US bombing missions
on crowded areas further stoked
anger and drew new recruits to
extremist organizations. "Every
village raid, every drone strike,
and every shot fired in anger on

> "In countries that have been invaded and bombed, some people thirst for bloody revenge."[65]
>
> —Stephen Kinzer, journalist and author

foreign soil produces anti-Western passion. Some are shocked
when that passion leads to violent reaction. They should not be,"
writes Stephen Kinzer. "In countries that have been invaded and
bombed, some people thirst for bloody revenge."[65]

The very understandable desire to hunt down and kill or capture a terrorist in the Middle East has been thus met with the
equally understandable anger of someone whose family member is killed by a stray bomb. Terrorists have used the suffering
resulting from war to recruit more terrorists. It becomes an endless cycle—a terrorist attack triggers a military response, which in
turn unleashes violence that leads to more terrorism. "We cannot
use force everywhere that a radical ideology takes root," noted
President Barack Obama in 2013, "and in the absence of a strategy that reduces the wellspring of extremism, a perpetual war—
through drones or Special Forces or troop deployments—will
prove self-defeating, and alter our country in troubling ways."[66]

Propaganda and the Lone Wolf

The self-defeating nature of the war on terror indicates that the
approach has completely failed to stop the spread of Islamist ideology. Islamist ideology's rapid spread around the globe demon-
strates that the extremists have been winning the war of ideas.
The evidence for this lies in the fact that the war on terror has been
so successful militarily but has made little difference in the spread
of Islamist extremism. The fiery messages of Islamist extremism
are now heard all over the world through the Internet. By gorging

on an endless diet of online propaganda, a terrorist can be born without ever leaving the house and without ever having met an Islamist in person. Indeed, virtual recruiting has become the foremost tool of terror groups. "They are virtual coaches who are providing guidance and encouragement through the process—from radicalization to recruitment into a specific plot,"[67] says terrorism expert Nathaniel Barr.

The spread of online propaganda has resulted in a spate of terrorist attacks that are generally carried out by just one person or a couple of people—and are often referred to as lone wolf attacks. These self-radicalized extremists act as time bombs in their own countries, nursing their anger and waiting to explode. "Again and again since 9/11 terror attacks in the West have been carried out by second-generation Muslims who are citizens of the very country they are attacking," writes terrorism expert Peter Bergen. "This is also a key reason that they are sometimes so hard to detect or to stop. These terrorists are not interlopers from other lands—but rather our neighbors."[68]

Military successes in the war on terror have only inspired more terrorism. Islamist extremists have gotten the upper hand in the struggle because they have more effectively spread their ideas. As a result, the war on terror has been counterproductive and cannot be judged a success.

Source Notes

Chapter One: A Brief History of Islamist Extremism

1. Quoted in Dana Adams Schmidt, "Egyptian Premier Is Slain by Cairo Student Terrorist," *New York Times*, December 29, 1948, p. 1. www.nytimes.com.
2. Quoted in Joseph S. Spoerl, "The World View of Hasan al-Banna and the Muslim Brotherhood," *New English Review*, December 2012. www.newenglishreview.org.
3. *Economist*, "The Father of Islamic Fundamentalism: Portrait of a Revolutionary," June 15, 2010. www.economist.com.
4. Jayshree Bajoria, "Egypt's Muslim Brotherhood," *Huffington Post*, February 3, 2011. www.huffingtonpost.com.
5. Quoted in William Claiborne, "Millions Welcome Khomeini to Iran: Throngs Give Khomeini Tumultuous Welcome in Tehran," *Washington Post*, February 1, 1979. www.washingtonpost.com.
6. Mark Bowden, "Among the Hostage-Takers," *Atlantic*, December 2004. www.theatlantic.com.
7. Quoted in Ruth Alexander and Hannah Moore, "Are Most Victims of Terrorism Muslim?," BBC News, January 20, 2015. www.bbcnews.com.
8. Rukmini Callimachi et al., "'An Endless War': Why 4 U.S. Soldiers Died in a Remote African Desert," *New York Times*, February 20, 2018. www.nytimes.com.

Chapter Two: Is Islamist Extremism the Result of Political Repression?

9. Jessica Stern, "What Motivates Terrorists?," Hoover Institution, January 21, 2011. www.hoover.org.
10. Quoted in Jack Shenker and Brian Whitaker, "The Muslim Brotherhood Uncovered," *Guardian* (Manchester), February 8, 2011. www.theguardian.com.
11. Quoted in Paul Crompton, "King Farouk's Fabulous Wealth," Al Arabiya News, January 30, 2014. http://english.alarabiya.net.

12. *Economist*, "Egypt's Rulers: A History Lesson," February 3, 2014. www.economist.com.
13. Brian Till, "A Note on Egyptian Torture," *Atlantic*, February 1, 2011. www.theatlantic.com.
14. Suzanne Maloney, "Iran Primer: The Revolutionary Economy," *Frontline*, PBS, October 26, 2010. www.pbs.org.
15. David Patrikarakos, "The Last Days of Iran Under the Shah," *FT Magazine*, February 6, 2009. www.ft.com.
16. Quoted in Parisa Hafezi, "Life in Iran Under the Shah and Now," Reuters, June 11, 2009. www.reuters.com.
17. Jonathan C. Randal, "SAVAK Jails Stark Reminder of Shah's Rule," *Washington Post*, January 13, 1979. www.washington post.com.
18. Daniel Byman, "State Sponsor of Terror: The Global Threat of Iran," testimony of Daniel Byman before the House Committee on Foreign Affairs Subcommittee on Terrorism, Nonproliferation, and Trade, Brookings Institution, February 11, 2015. www.brookings.edu.
19. Daniel Brogan, "Al Qaeda's Greeley Roots: How the Intellectual Father of Osama Bin Laden's Terrorist Network Learned to Hate America in a Tiny Colorado Town," *5280*, June/July 2003. www.5280.com.
20. David Von Drehle, "A Lesson in Hate: How an Egyptian Student Came to Study 1950s America and Left Determined to Wage Holy War," *Smithsonian*, February 2006. www.smith sonianmag.com.
21. Quoted in Mark Weston, *Prophets and Princes: Saudi Arabia from Muhammad to the Present*. Hoboken, NJ: Wiley, 2008, p. 364.
22. Patrick Kingsley, "How Mohamed Morsi, Egypt's First Elected President, Ended Up on Death Row," *Guardian* (Manchester), June 1, 2015. www.theguardian.com.
23. Quoted in Raymond H. Anderson, "Ayatollah Ruhollah Khomeini, 89, Relentless Founder of Iran's Islamic Republic," *New York Times*, June 5, 1989. www.nytimes.com.
24. Quoted in Kristen McTighe, "Years of Torture in Iran Come to Light," *New York Times*, November 21, 2012. www.nytimes.com.
25. Karim Sadjadpour, "The Battle for Iran," *Atlantic*, December 31, 2017. www.theatlantic.com.

Chapter Three: Has Western Intervention in the Middle East Caused Islamist Extremism?

26. Quoted in Carol Rosenberg, "Alleged Mastermind Tells Obama 9/11 Was America's Fault," *Miami Herald*, February 8, 2017. www.miamiherald.com.

27. Quoted in Robin Wright, "How the Curse of the Sykes-Picot Agreement Still Haunts the Middle East," *New Yorker*, April 30, 2016. www.newyorker.com.

28. Bernard Lewis, "The Revolt of Islam," *New Yorker*, November 19, 2001. www.newyorker.com.

29. Richard Cottam, "Goodbye to America's Shah," *Foreign Policy*, March 16, 1979. www.foreignpolicy.com.

30. Samuel P. Huntington, "The Clash of Civilizations?," *Foreign Affairs*, Summer 1993, p. 32.

31. Robert Fisk, "Why We Reject the West—by Osama bin Laden," *Independent* (London), May 17, 2016. www.independent.co.uk.

32. Reuel Marc Gerecht, "The Gospel According to Osama bin Laden," *Atlantic*, January 2002. www.theatlantic.com.

33. Rohan Gunaratna, "Al Qaeda's Ideology," Hudson Institute, May 19, 2015. www.hudson.org.

34. Eli Lake, "Muslims Are Often the First Victims of Muslim Terrorists," Bloomberg, November 24, 2017. www.bloomberg.com.

35. Jacob Poushter, "Support for al Qaeda Was Low Before (and After) Osama bin Laden's Death," Pew Research Center, May 2, 2014. www.pewcenter.org.

36. Quoted in Katie Engelhart, "Revealing Quilliam, the Muslim Destroyers of the English Far Right," *Vice*, October 10, 2013. www.vice.com.

37. Quoted in Patrick Wintour, "Boris Johnson Blames 'Crack Cocaine of Jihadi Terrorism' on Repressive States," *Guardian* (Manchester), December 6, 2017. www.theguardian.com.

Chapter Four: Does Poverty Cause Islamist Extremism?

38. Quoted in Jake Harriman, "Linking Extreme Poverty and Global Terrorism," *New York Times*, March 13, 2012. www.nytimes.com.

39. UNICEF, "At Least One in Four Children Live in Poverty in the Middle East and North Africa," press release, May 15, 2017. www.unicef.org.
40. FATA Research Centre, *Extremism and Radicalization: An Overview of the Social, Political, Cultural and Economic Landscape of the FATA*. Islamabad, Pakistan: FATA Research Centre, 2012. frc.com.pk.
41. Kartika Bhatia and Hafez Ghanem, "Report: How Do Education and Unemployment Affect Support for Violent Extremism? Evidence from Eight Arab Countries," Brookings Institution, March 22, 2017. www.brookings.edu.
42. Quoted in Ahmed El Amraoui, "Tunisia's Ghannouchi: Poverty Is a Root Cause of Terror," Al Jazeera, November 14, 2015. www.aljazeera.com.
43. Quoted in Mike Eckel and Harun Maruf, "'Why He Chose to Leave This Good Land?' Islamic State Beckons and Somali Americans Again Struggle with Radicalization," Voice of America. https://projects.voanews.com.
44. Jake Harriman, "Linking Extreme Poverty and Global Terrorism," *New York Times*, March 13, 2012. www.nytimes.com.
45. Quoted in Mark Townsend, "ISIS Paying Smugglers' Fees in Recruitment Drive Among Child Refugees," *Guardian* (Manchester), February 4, 2017. www.theguardian.com.
46. James A. Piazza, "Rooted in Poverty? Terrorism, Poor Economic Development, and Social Cleavages," *Terrorism and Political Violence*, 2006, p. 170.
47. Lawrence Wright, "The Man Behind Bin Laden," *New Yorker*, September 16, 2002. www.newyorker.com.
48. Fouad Ajami, "Islam's Nowhere Men," *Wall Street Journal*, May 10, 2010. www.wsj.com.
49. David Berreby, "Engineering Terror," *New York Times Magazine*, September 10, 2010. www.nytimes.com.
50. *Economist*, "Exploding Misconceptions: Alleviating Poverty May Not Reduce Terrorism but Could Make It Less Effective," December 16, 2010. www.economist.com.
51. Alan B. Krueger and Jitka Malecková, "Does Poverty Cause Terrorism?," *New Republic*, June 24, 2002. www.newrepublic.com.
52. Alan Krueger, "What Makes a Terrorist," American Enterprise Institute, November 7, 2007. www.aei.org.

Chapter Five: Has the War on Terror Been Successful?

53. Brian Michael Jenkins, "Fifteen Years On, Where Are We in the 'War on Terror'?," *CTC Sentinel*, September 7, 2016. https://ctc.usma.edu.
54. Suzanne Daley, "After the Attacks: The Alliance; For the First Time, NATO Invokes Joint Defense Pact with U.S.," *New York Times*, September 13, 2001. www.nytimes.com.
55. Michael E. O'Hanlon, "A Flawed Masterpiece (Afghanistan Conflict 2001–)," *Foreign Affairs*, May–June 2002, p. 47.
56. Terry McDermott and Josh Meyer, "Inside the Mission to Catch Khalid Sheikh Mohammed," *Atlantic*, April 2, 2012. www.theatlantic.com.
57. Quoted in Daniel Halper, "Obama Defiantly Declares 'Al Qaeda Is on Its Heels,' Even After Successful Terrorist Attacks," *Weekly Standard*, October 9, 2012. www.weeklystandard.com.
58. Quoted in Andrew England, "Iraq Announces Defeat of ISIS," *Financial Times* (London), December 9, 2017. www.ft.com.
59. White House, *National Strategy for Counterterrorism*, June 28, 2011. https://obamawhitehouse.archives.gov.
60. Stephen Kinzer, "Blame the West's Interventions for Today's Terrorism," *Boston Globe*, November 24, 2015. www.bostonglobe.com.
61. Graeme Wood, "True Believers: How ISIS Made Jihad Religious Again," *Foreign Affairs*, September/October 2017, p. 136.
62. Tom Englehardt, "Mapping a World from Hell," January 4, 2018. *TomDispatch.com* (blog). www.tomdispatch.com.
63. Agence France-Presse, "French Forces Kill at Least 10 Extremists in Mali: Military Sources," *National* (Abu Dhabi, United Arab Emirates), February 15, 2018. www.thenational.ae.
64. Quoted in Valerie Volcovici, "U.S. Senators Seek Answers on U.S. Presence in Niger After Ambush," Reuters, October 22, 2017. www.reuters.com.
65. Kinzer, "Blame the West's Interventions for Today's Terrorism."
66. Quoted in Sean Illing, "How America's 'War on Terror' Was (Unwittingly) Designed to Last Forever," Vox, January 6, 2017. www.vox.com.
67. Quoted in Rukmini Callimachi, "Not 'Lone Wolves' After All: How ISIS Guides World's Terror Plots from Afar," *New York Times*, February 4, 2017. www.nytimes.com.
68. Peter Bergen, "Bergen: A Pattern in Terror—Second Generation, Homegrown," CNN, May 24, 2017. www.cnn.com.

For Further Research

Books

Michael Axworthy, *Revolutionary Iran: A History of the Islamic Republic*. Oxford, UK: Oxford University Press, 2013.

Andrew Bacevich, *America's War for the Greater Middle East: A Military History*. New York: Random House, 2016.

Steve Coll, *Ghost Wars: The Secret History of the CIA, Afghanistan, and Bin Laden, from the Soviet Invasion to September 10, 2001*. New York: Penguin, 2004.

Rex A. Hudson, *Who Becomes a Terrorist and Why?* New York: Skyhorse, 2018.

Ed Husain, *The Islamist: Why I Left Radical Islam*. London: Penguin, 2007.

Nathan Lean, *Understanding Islam and the West*. New York: Rowman & Littlefield International, 2018.

Souad Mekhennet, *I Was Told to Come Alone: My Journey Behind the Lines of Jihad*. New York: Holt, 2017.

Lawrence Wright, *The Looming Tower: Al-Qaeda and the Road to 9/11*. New York: Knopf, 2006.

Malala Yousafzai and Patricia McCormick, *I Am Malala: How One Girl Stood Up for Education and Changed the World*. Boston: Little, Brown, 2014.

Websites

Federal Bureau of Investigation (www.fbi.gov). The FBI's website contains news on recent terrorist threats and links to terrorism-related government websites.

Global Terrorism Database (www.start.umd.edu/gtd). This searchable database, operated by the University of Maryland, includes information on terrorist attacks all over the world.

Quilliam Foundation (www.quilliaminternational.com). This counterextremism organization was started by former Islamists who now offer programs to combat extremism. The website includes links to publications and to video discussions of issues concerning extremism.

Roots of Terrorism Teaching Guide, *Frontline* (www.pbs.org /wgbh/pages/frontline/teach/terror). Public television's investigative series *Frontline* provides terrorism-related information for teachers and students on its website and links to *Frontline* episodes related to the subject.

September 11th Sourcebooks, National Security Archive (https://nsarchive2.gwu.edu//NSAEBB/sept11/index.html). A vast collection of declassified primary documents from the National Security Archive, including reports on the Taliban, terrorist groups, and US policies.

Index

poverty rate in, 43
Minnesota, Islamist extremists in, 45–46
Mohammed, Khalid Sheikh, 30, 58
Morsi, Mohamed, 25–26, **26**
Mosaddegh, Mohammad, 32
Mubarak, Hosni, 25
Muslim Brotherhood
  army and, after overthrow of Farouk, 24–25
  beliefs of, 9
  founding of, 9, 17, 29
  as Freedom and Justice Party, 25
  influence on al Qaeda, 10
  outlawed, 17, 19, 26
  in power in Egypt, 25–26, **26**
  prior to radicalization, 17–18
  turn to violence
    during army rule of Egypt, 25
    assassination of Nuqrashi and, 8–9
    attempted assassination of Nasser, 10, 19
    chief advocate of, 23
    under Farouk's regime, 17–18
    radicalization process, 18–19, **19**
Muslims
  lack of support for al Qaeda, 39
  as majority of victims of Islamist extremism, 13, 35, 37–38, **38**
  peaceful coexistence of, with non-Muslims in West, 39–40

Nasser, Gamal Abdel, 10, 18, 19
National Counterterrorism Center, 13
National Strategy for Counterterrorism (US intelligence community), 60
Nemati, Iraj, 21

New York Times (newspaper), 14, 56
Niger, 64
North Atlantic Treaty Organization (NATO), 56
Northern Alliance, **57**, 57–58
Norton, Ben, 29
Nuqrashi, Mahmud Fahmi al-, 8

Obama, Barack, 48, 59, 65
O'Hanlon, Michael E., 58
Operation Barkhane, 64

Pahlavi, Mohammad Rerza (shah of Iran), 11–12, 20
Pakistan, 43–44, 58
Patrikarakos, David, 20–21
Pew Research Center, 39
Philippines, 63
Piazza, James A., 49
political oppression
  absence of, does not mean absence of extremism, 22
  is main cause of Islamist extremism, 15
    applied when citizens protest unjust conditions, 16–17
    forcing of protest movements underground, 17–18, 20–21
    prison radicalization and, **19**, 19–20, 21
  is not main cause of Islamist extremism, 15
    does not wane when Islamists are in power, 25–27, **26**
    does not wane when Islamists are not repressed, 24–25
    rejection of Western way of life has caused extremism, 23–24
    standard radicalization model does not exist, 22
Poushter, Jacob, 39

Picture Credits

About the Author

Robert Green has been writing about the politics of Hong Kong and Taiwan for the Economist Intelligence Unit and Oxford Analytica for more than a decade. He holds a master's degree in journalism from New York University and a master's degree in area studies from Harvard University. He enjoys writing, above all, about history.